CW00968284

# Responses to *Forbidden Colours* (1988) by Felix Gonzalez-Torres

## Pilot Press
London

# Forbidden colours: a question to the reader

My country recognized Palestine as a state in 2010.

Decree 1882, signed by the president and the chancellor consists of only two articles.

Article 1: "Palestine is recognized as a free and independent state",

Article 2: "the Ministry of Foreign Affairs, International Trade and Worship shall adopt the necessary measures for the fulfillment of the provisions of the preceding article".

The countries bordering my country, and the ones I like to go to the most, also recognized Palestine as a state: Brazil, Uruguay and Paraguay.

Does your country recognize Palestine as a sovereign state?

and

can you imagine what it would be like to live undocumented in your own country?

Cecilia Pavòn

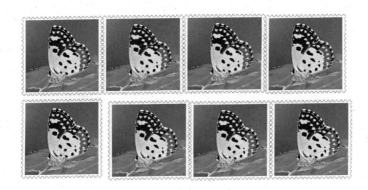

Ben Estes

## Palestinian Embroidery
## (Kettle's Yard, 19 October 2023)

if you prick
needle gives
the eye of need
under & reseen

each bright
a dyeing
rose & madder
linen literature

steel bites white
welling red
the letters P, L
& O stitched

on the hips
worn closer
than posters
or graffiti

harder to unpick

So Mayer

# Black White Red and Green

The famous expression Zionists like to use about Israel that it is a land without people for a people without a land is perfectly true (linguistically) in the sense that Palestinians have been thought of as a moveable obstruction beginning in the 19th century by the first conceiver of Zionism and their pals the British and as we moved into the 20th century Palestinians have been legally entirely erased from consideration since 1917, starting with the Balfour Declaration and the League of Nations Mandate for Palestine in 1922 and from then on, persistently, in every public statement, agreement, Security Council Resolution put forth by involved parties meaning Israel and the British, the French and eventually the US and all of the west's client Arab countries, everyone has, for almost a century now, maintained in all possible ways that Palestine and Palestinians do not exist except as terrorists. I mean that's sick shit, right. Also it is pretty queer. For a while now I have had this growing impulse to say that I am Palestinian. I feel I was born a stalwart for their cause and my feeling was reinforced, wildly, by a trip I took there in 2017 (through a group called PalFest) when I saw the Palestinian condition with my own eyes. Palestinians are daily denied their most fervent wish which is to live – to simply have rights, a home, and a right to return to it and I woke up today in this worst of all times, during this genocidal moment, a whole hog attempt on the part of Israel and the US to eradicate finally and at last these "non-existent" Palestinians from Gaza and meanwhile Israel is maiming, arresting and killing Palestinians in the West Bank too. This naked moment in terms of the western powers and Israel's utterly armed and activated contempt for the people of Palestine is making me think and feel many things but I woke today, looked at my phone and I just began to cry looking at babies laid out in little white cotton funeral bags, dead children's heads bouncing on the shoulders of devastated adults who still held them in ambulances, adults who cannot bear what they are obviously bearing. A woman screaming for a long while at the camera. She was saying so much more than WTF. They are crying, I am crying, a kid is crying for his mother, a girl screams for her father, her siblings and her mother. They have been pulled out of collapsed buildings and their parents and their siblings didn't make it out alive and it is simply the worse thing I've ever seen and for them, my brothers and sisters, my parents, my friends, my fellow humans it is the worst thing they have ever seen and they have seen things that should not be part of daily life for anyone and it has been part of their daily life for seventy five years. I won't apologize for this being a repetition of what you already know. Sometimes the facts are so mind-blowing that all you can do is repeat them. These conditions are an awful chant. An evil poem. My country is arming Israel steadily, my country is refusing to support the ceasefire proposal at the UN, the US (which is not *us*, but also devastatingly, it is) is the only country vetoing the proposal so in a way since this is not land that Americans will ever need to live on except for those Palestinian Americans who want to go home or an American who might decide they wanted to live there but the latter is probably pretty rare - but America, my point, doesn't *need* this land. Israel thinks they do so in the sense that striking someone and striking them harder than the more involved party (Israel) ever could and ever will and I mean we all know that pretty much all the weapons Israel is using were supplied by us, so to my mind the greater crime is our crime. Our American crime. Red white and blue crime, right here. It's kind of like our dick is committing this crime, doubly wrong, immoral, deeply obscene. We don't need the land. Our need is strategic, i.e. pornographic. When a rich man who has enough for 100 lives still has to accumulate more and more - and where are they getting the wealth from, from the poor obviously, from somebody else's labor, siphoning off from someone else's land, off their ideas and creativity, off their sex, it is capitalism at its most repugnant, capitalism as addictive sport, capitalism unto death and will the people you are using die first or will you yourself keel over in a seizure of overexcitement from digging your snout deeper into the earth than anything living ever could and so you die of this horrible feeding, this is what is currently bringing my country down, a hideous horrible rapacious greed. Greed for power, greed over a bad idea, greed for cozy and consumptive racism, greed for declaring (me too!) that the other is NOT while your actions are in fact causing them grievous, unimaginable, intolerable pain. It's the greed of the torturer. I suppose I'm Palestinian because of all the ways I've long felt *I'm* not. I won't list my qualities that don't "count" and don't "matter" but as we know there are bodies that matter and bodies that don't and Palestinians don't matter and I don't. I keep thinking of Judith Butler's idea about the lesbian phallus. I'll get this wrong I'll promise you but the idea is something to the effect that bodies flicker, are material and not. And language ultimately makes them exist somehow and the phallus is language itself, maybe the law, and the phallus is not actually male, not the penis, at all, (though "he" acts like that's true) not the dick so actually anyone can have a phallus in fact, if not a penis and Butler attributes the extra desire, the kind of transgressive excitement around for instance (her instance) homosexual and transgender desire that is increasingly banned actually winds up making them, us, I, myself, exist even more attractive and lively in that all the excitement around wanting us to stop, to just go away, to not use the bathroom, to not let our kids choose what gender they are, it somehow is the most hot and exciting thing today in the greedy hungry bowels of America the perpetrator and certainly since the 60s - when Palestine's fortunes plummeted - after the 1967 war they went lower than ever before, at that moment Palestine became a righteous cause - for themselves and the world. People saw and understood inside and outside of Palestine that you cannot talk the body (a people) away because half of it is invisible and half of it is that pulsing vital and exciting thing (much more than that thing that is trying to kill it) and all of Israel's happy statements that they are about to finish the work of the Nakba have never been less true because the beating Palestinian heart and the world's growing capacity to know it at last and to finally comprehend the extent of the injustice they have incurred for almost a century at the hands of Israel and the western powers and complicit Arab countries has to do with their deep human attachment to the experience and the knowledge that this is their home, their history, they cannot ever be stopped and they will not die, and America probably will, though we kill and kill and kill them.

Eileen Myles

# Away

Equality
Struggling to encompass
Day being
Absorbing light energy.

Station for evaporation
Sea sponge inked
Rinsing in rain
Anthropomorphism.

In action
I am
We are
Free.

To walk earth
We came from sea
Wet footprints
Orient path.

Dissolved
Into the atmosphere
They fall on us again
Our bodies feet.

Paul Lee

## To a home which is not

To be remembered for your depletion: do you
bet on it? Can you even pray against it?
She never said it was beautiful.
It was a weapon.

Sorrow cascades through grief but doesn't
make up the meat of it, which refuses anyways.
She never said it was beautiful. Nothing to
make sense of, no way to cascade this
sorrow, the rain that fell

One wall was one thing. Another black. Who cares?
It isn't the heart of the thing. Throw yourself
against it, see what happens. See what happens,
what happens now.

Life cascades through sorrow like death, won't quit.
What's grief? You throw a rock at the wall. It
sticks. What's left

The last morning glory gaped and grasped its last
breath. Whose hands toiled richly? Whose hands
fumbled poorly down into the topsoil wet still
with the year's stasis and change?

The buckets empty. The water still. There was an arch:
one to pass through and one to lie down under,
rain on the stones still saying stay,
stay here awhile.

So we stay and so we stayed, and made a life: so
long, so still. Still warm, that's all. In another
life the eye gaped with sight.
Now it aches, too much light.

We never said it was beautiful. The light was.
The sun—

jimmy cooper

# Obsessive compulsive destruction

The compulsion to repeat the cycle of violence the compulsion to repeat the cycle of violence the repetition of compulsive violence the repetition of convulsing violence the repetition of violence is beyond belief splintering worlds splintering worlds as we speak of nothing but parity of the right to protect to defend to attack to eradicate to destroy through weapons of mass destruction mass destruction destruction en masse weapons that need to be destructed en masse weapons turned on civilisations en masse civilians en masse children en masse killing indiscriminately killing deliberately en masse is genocide is genocide by any other name anything less than the deliberate killing of thousands the deliberate killing of millions is genocide genocide by any other name is genocide genocide by no name is happening watched by the western world named as defence protection retaliation a right not wrong a right far right to kill humans with weapons man-made weapons state made state weapons bought with legal tender cold hard cash currency currently dropping on millions civilians en masse children en masse genocide is happening while we watch while we look away genocide is happening while we look away from the repetition of convulsing violence convulsive repulsive violence violence breeds violence repeats repeats repeats

Lucy Swan

Davide Meneghello

## In a particular order

The first notes of a howl
enter your heart like a swallow
and makes a nest with your lover's hair

I made it so it could be seen
I made it so it could be heard
it remains unseen
it remains unheard

like a cry in the dirt
I cannot hold you
my limbs are gone

as if they have been blown off in this war
the radio silent
my bed empty
of you.

Chris Jones

# Arrows

*Guard: Are you crying?*

*Natacha: No, because it's forbidden.*

In Jean-Luc Godard's 1965 film *Alphaville*, he presents a city where passion, emotion, love and poetry are forbidden. We are shown the spectacle of violence as nothing but glib entertainment where men and women are executed during synchronized swimming performances.

The city is controlled by an omnipotent computer. The city has become a computer. It is controlled by totalitarian machines. It streets are filled with arrows. The arrow is the key symbol for this world because it directs human thought and action. It negates the individual mind. There can be no meandering because that would be illogical. The arrow is the logic of death.

There is a room where a girl is crying. The guard cannot understand her tears because these are forbidden. A poem is being read through a machine in the wall: *Despair has no wings, nor does love... No face, they do not speak... I don't look at them... I don't speak to them... But I am as alive as my love and despair...*

Matthew Kinlin and Neil Davies

I begin re-reading *Un Captif Amoureux* and someone calls it a memoir that is a bomb. I walk to B&Q with you and feel my language leaking out of me: it is ensconced in the cold drive to put my body on the line.

Things are so far gone and the goalposts have moved so utterly that it's easy to believe people can no longer say things with their full throat. There is false-nuance and there is generalised antipathy and there is pausing in McDonald's, watching a line cook who can't be older than sixteen, and remembering your own first gauntlet of shift work, its depersonalisation.

I come back to Genet for a lot of things. For starting again and for looking long. For invoking what Edward Said called "an utterly undomesticated sensibility", and it's this sensibility which I reinscribe repeatedly into my body as I read, because it is a gesture of decolonisation. In that reading I again begin the shedding of good sense, respectability, moral relativism, civility, deference, all conformities; of gender and thiefdom; carceral logics and hierarchies of violence, apologia, bourgeois syntax; arbitrary distances. All that separates you from anyone else is a splinter in the thumb.

Like everyone in a very particular circle I read the Fred Moten quote, *"I just need you to realise that this shit is killing you, too, however much more softly, you stupid motherfucker, you know?"* and remember, with guilt, that I have grown a crust to survive, like shellac, like always, and that this crust is antithetical to a politics of coalition. It's a long brindled slug of a scab and it yawns open with new picking, but better – always – to be inflamed and tingling. Because guilt without action is worse than apathy, and unforgivably inert.

Really the choices are: spiral into a mire of complicity or hack a wedge out of yourself. Nothing else matters but the hinge of an arm.

In a throng of three hundred thousand people I begin crying uncontrollably. You both wait for me and we begin walking together, solemn at first. Like you can't catch the breath in your throat. Soon downpour and haze fill the street to its brim while the Met's helicopters squat over everything, like ticks on a lens. They've come to feed. Or just harvest faces. How far away can you pick us out from? Can you triangulate the snarl of a lip, hooded eyes, a grimace? Do my streaming tears help identify me? I cry in public a lot. The helicopters are matte black and circle like carrion reversed; down here we're the bugs animating the kill's skin.

*Yes you fucker I know you're on top, don't worry.*

I've covered my face but feel it boring into me all the same. That impossible scrutiny and latent militance. True anonymity is unworkable, and as a deviant woman I strive for it, but still under its gaze I'm made naked, and so begin shedding all of it, suddenly: the ossification, the rain, the grief as it accretes, the chronic poison of my phone and everything steeled since 2019. My body, deemed deviant, that Genet shores up; the deemed deviance of a people fleeing genocide that Genet dwelled within, for all that time. Who marked us both for death?

This might sound trite but I mean it with the deepest feeling: it's not reductive to be rocked by a sudden and seamless awareness of the world's indivisible violence, as it is writ upon you and upon everyone else. Genet lived his life knotting it all together – tracing the interstices, running his fingers over each aperture. The wounds. There are no separate struggles for liberation, that's the lesson of vagrancy; what being criminalised teaches you.

Because the same machines and systems are already coming for all of us. Since before our parent's parents. Call it what you want: imperial core, common-wealth, holocaust, sectarianism, apartheid, landlord, Pinkerton, brownshirt, black and tan, pro-life, Stop the Boats, stop and search, No DSS, section 21, waiting list, Clean Coal, three strikes, both sides, common sense, urban renewal, ASBO, Prevent, Mumsnet, capitalist white supremacist heteropatriarchy, "we know what a woman is".

Fascism, we know, has no logic and so it cannot be unmade by logic. Only by feeling. By which I mean that I'm glad that you're here with me, walking, at this threshold where language begins to break down, numbed by the violence of a thousand vertices, before swelling again in unison. Together, here on the street. Together at the same moment that your deviant body is being offered the chance to begin again, just as mine has, and so we hide it, under our clothes – from the police and from our comrades today and under the blank eye of the helicopters.

We are not wired to comprehend this but we have to try. Fascism resists language because it destroys meaning, but nothing is beyond is expression. That was another lesson you taught me.

If we are all only writing about our inability to write, if we are able to write only about transfixion, paralysis, then really we deserve to write nothing at all. There's the tip of the spear and then there's this. There's lingering and there's being backed into a corner and then there's this. The page. The page which is empty, or filled only by words which allude to an inarticulable horror – which might as well be a sea of guilt, thick and indulgent.

Chris Kraus said Simone Weil was wracked by a 'panic of altruism', which we might read as a grappling with her own complicity; the relative comfort of her class. When I think of Weil, I can't shake the image of her squinting short-sighted down the irons of a rifle, shoulder-to-breast with the Durutti Column, taking aim at one of Franco's bombers; the blazing sun glints off the barrel, she fumbles the trigger, and misses. Later she would burn herself on a cooking fire and be asked to leave. Her parents had to come and collect her.

This vision of Weil's incompetence is clearly some kind of internalised miso-gyny, or rather the incorrect assumption that she was a revolutionary of the mind only, because still she threw her meagre body against danger, over and over; even in hunger and voluntary repatriation, after her mother and father had fled to America. But still what she sought was sacrifice, not death. To use her body as a tool.

Simone, born with everything, sought poverty out, its every permutation, in rapture. Not quite a comrade but something more expiatory. Genet, born with nothing, sought out struggles for liberation across the globe. No longer a convict but something more fugitive.

Like Weil we have to tease out our own inadequacy to dispense with it. Like Genet we have to know our own contradictions to go beyond them. This isn't a shedding of your own positionality or becoming ambiguated, I'm not even sure that's useful. Simply that we have to begin with our own grief.

Hesse K.

Prem Sahib

## Postdiluvian

After the flood, he pulls out
like a retreating army; a horse
rode hard and put away wet.

*Adelphopoiesis* means *brother-making*,
means there was something analogous
to marriage even for faggots of the faith,

even though Sodom and Gomorrah
was a sting operation, even so;
sin isn't a stain on the soul—

it's more like the stain on glass
that filters light through the windows.
There are no trespassers in the Holy Land

except Zionist warmongers. I saw missiles
hit news buildings, shells of white phosphorous
shot by IDF artillery—they drop like a rain of fire;

o myth of justifiable violence, philosophers
debate the fairness of disproportionate response
in forums while the world is quiet. O the Hague's

hypocrisy, I thought we were all God's children,
how Jesus is a prophet in Islam too; I knew he's not
in Judaism but why would he be, Jewish people

were subjugated under Christian monarchies.
What Freire called *sub-oppression*: the oppressed
becoming oppressors, straying from liberation,

deviation on the path to enlightenment.
Any war is immoral. Anyone who calls war
*holy* is a criminal. If someone says

there's something
you can't talk about,
you should.

William Butler

# Book Colour Theory

Cocteau had his *White Book*. Mao his *Little Red Book*. Jung had a much bigger heavier *Red Book*. Muammar Gaddafi had his emerald or would you say forest *Green Book*. Daniil Kharms had his *Blue Notebook*. Alexander Vvedensky had a *Gray Notebook*. Heidegger had his *Black Notebooks*. Dylan his *Red* and *Blue Spiral Notebooks*. Roger Casement had his *Black Diaries* and his *White Diaries*. Wittgenstein his *Blue* and his *Brown* and his *Yellow* and his *Pink Book* oh the *Pink Book*.

To summarize: some of these books are very long books, refer to Heidegger's 1000 plus pages; some are very short books, compare this to Kharms' 14pp.

Some of these books are political tracts, while others are of a philosophical or personal nature; some are full of revelations and dreams and visions; some are full of erotic encounters and forbidden thoughts and pleasures; some are full of little stories and poems and songs; some are full of complex ideological and agrarian and economic systems; some are full of psychotic episodes and unravelings, indefensible affinities and untenable ideas.

Some of these books are bound in silk or onionskin or cloth or oilcloth or leather; some of their covers are shiny and others are matte; some are written carefully and tinily or carelessly in the author's hand, within thin horizontal lines or the broad columns of ledgers; some typed reverently or blurrily by the hands of others; some are riddled with errors; some were used as evidence of genius, some were used as evidence of degeneracy; some led directly or indirectly to the author's death at the hands of the state (Casement, treason:noose;Kharms,counterrevolutionary:starvation;Vvede nsky,counterrevolutionary: pleurisy?); some of these books were lost and some are still missing and some were found; some have been collated, some are as is, some have been digitized, some have been archived under very cold conditions; some were photographed or mimeographed, the ink forced through a machine onto paper like ideas forced through one's body onto the page; some were published anonymously and some were published posthumously; some circulated widely, some distributed in a restricted, clandestine manner; some of these books were not intended for publication, were not meant to be perceived by anyone's eyes other than the author's (must research the possible connection between colour of authors' eyes and colour of their books.)

Yet: all these books, no matter their colour, their intentionality, their aura, or their reception, are the disordered, disjointed ramblings of arguably and variably disordered and disjointed individuals. Men, genitally speaking, with too many ideas in their heads, too many fantasies, too many secrets, too many images bursting to get out. Hence the strict necessity of the delimiting yet generous phenomenon of *the book*, a form delirious, yet systematic, where we may contain all our ideas into some kind of bound system.

So the question remains: is my book a private or public document? Tell me, unknown reader, inside the confines of this book, how much or how little shall I reveal to you, that is to say, what will I be able to hide and what will I be unable to conceal? You see the colour of my book keeps changing, as I'm dreaming of a book that will evade the eternal censors, and although Wittgenstein pointed out that ordinary language is unable to describe a particular shade of colour and there is no criterion to recognize a colour, please my handsome reader, whose eyes keep changing their colour, who is already reading this book although it remains to be finished, a book with which I will never see eye to eye, assist me with the question that I am pondering, the question that is most pressing: what colour is my book?

Alistair McCartney

Richard Porter

1.

Blessed is the tree which grows low next to the fence.
Blessed is the concrete. Blessed is the December rain,
which washes away the blood. Blessed is the wind which
moves the tear gas. Blessed is a burning bin. Blessed is
the ashtray on Maria's kitchen table. Blessed are the
stray cats on Boumpoulinas street. Blessed is the
Polytechnio, the stink of rotting food and gasoline, the
cupboard full of [                    ] we couldn't find a
place to put, so we put them in your apartment. Thank
god your landlord never visited. Blessed is the second-
storey window the cleaning lady in Petralona jumped out
of to escape the man who had been raping her for four
hours. Blessed is the pink and silver glitter which we
stuck to the wall outside the store in Omonia when Zac
was killed. Blessed are the roses we laid out for the dead
which the bastards tore to shreds.

2.

I have checked you for concussion three times. We are
standing in the shade of a cedar tree, and I shine my
phone torch in your eye, shielding your face from the sun
that is dripping through the leaves. Three times you were
hit in the head by a nazi. I ask you to walk in a straight
line, and I tell you not to drink alcohol for the next 24
hours, and to go to A and E if you start to feel sick or
dizzy. I talk a lot when I'm nervous.

We only kissed twice, a year ago. I still dream about her
most nights. I dream that we are on the beach. We pick
pomegranates from someone's garden, and walk on
rocks barefoot down to the waves, below the water. It is
the night before they broke her ribs and locked her in a
room for two days with her sister because she called a
cop a pig. In the dream, we are swimming.

There is a crack in everything. There is a hunger you can
read about, but never know. You hold my hand once,
and never again.

Kathy Pendrill

# For what was lost in words

REDDK how long RED wREDll lREDvWHITE so RED jGREENst
wBLACKnt thREDs to bWHITE my mWHITEmory
hWHITErWHITE bWHITEforWHITE RED dREDWHITE.

RED BLACKm not goREDng to lWHITEBLACKvWHITE my
homWHITE, comWHITE whBLACKt mBLACKy.

My bREDggWHITEst rWHITEgrWHITEt REDs not kREDssREDng
thREDs onWHITE gGREENy.

HWHITE dREDWHITEd two dBLACKys bBLACKck.

WWHITE hBLACKd told how mGREENch wWHITE lREDkWHITE
WHITEBLACKch othWHITEr BLACKnd RED wBLACKs too shy to
kREDss lBLACKst tREDmWHITE.

HWHITE dREDWHITEd REDn thWHITE bombREDng.

RED thREDnk BLACK bREDg pBLACKrt of mWHITE
dREDWHITEd too.

BLACKnd soon RED wREDll bWHITE dWHITEBLACKd.

To YoGREENnGREENs, RED wREDll kREDss yoGREEN REDn
hWHITEBLACKvWHITEn.

Richard James Hall

## Solidarity with the Palestinian land and peoples

past, present,
future whose lives
and flag reach
in every direction
like sunrise.
Locate us
in the now,
be attentive
to us as we
wave like a hand
or wave as
an American
baseball stadium
of families, a wave
that circles the space
like water does a drain.
Or as an ocean
wave that crests
way out, arrives then
retreats. We chant
from the river
to the sea. Free.
A wave
of the push-
pull of life.
A smoothing of
divides with
life flow, a flood
from below,
a roof
of blue sky.
As above.
The flag reaches
forward,
too. Will exist
in the future.

Will be waved
in crowds,
pinned over
hearts, planted
in soil.
So many flags are
combinations of colours
that expose us
as lovers
believers seers
alive and you
are ancient kill
arrow trying to
confine existence
to soupçon. This
is not only a less-
on in history
but a lesson in futures
and presents in
the now this is life.
As if we didn't
know the children
are ours, whoever
and always.
Are you with heart,
sirs? Are you
with humanity
in your human
bodies, sirs?
The Palestinian flag waves
from a woman's
centre, the gut
part, where she gives
birth, sirs. What
do you lean
your ear against
when anticipating
life, sirs? The flag

you bomb
like you do a family
huddled together
for a portrait
reaches in
every direction,
multiplies and
is covering
the earth,
gathering life
from your
storm, somehow,
for her waving.

Ashleigh A. Allen

# All And Everyone (Demo)

It is the splitting sun of near dusk and
the sliver of the moon. It is the pouring
out of fatigue, the head turning side to
side to catch its own burning, its own
spentness. It is cortisol, a poem ending
with cortisol, stress, seen on a screen
while the morning sun lights itself like
a beacon, like a portal, holds itself
firmly. It is four thousand candles. It is
a death count reaching, reaching, and it
is Palestine—a boy says he dreams of
his mother eating bread. Come, now, it
is prepared: your own tongue splitting,
your oak tree and Spanish moss, auto-
harp and owl, mother and father,
bright red husk of magnolia like
lacquered blood. Your south a void, a
hymn. Press an olive between your
thumb and index finger and feel its
cool, smell its salt. Press your face to
the window and drag it across the
glassy pane. What else can I say to
bring you to this *it is, it is, it is?* A boy
is dreaming of his mother. I am
walking on Shepherd Street. A stranger
asks me what I'm listening to. What is
it he wants me to hear? I say a singer's
name and am surprised by my own
voice. We pass each other into night,
advance into another sun. At the
library, lips close, my lover reminds me
that we woke together yesterday. His

voice a charm, some spell bleeding into presence. *It is, it is.* A boy is dreaming. He tells us so as death surrounds. I pass a metal fence, a sign for a carnival affixed to it. A wooden painting displays a lion, its face cut out for a child's. The child, the boy, a lion. Overhead, the clouds are like mountains, the light an unreal glow. Here there's thunder and nothing's burning. I conjure every tree that's stunned me, conjure Ola Belle Reed's warbling and it's distorted by bomb, by drone, by plane. It's the boy's dream telling us what he's endured. It's the sprawl of bodies reaching, reaching. What it means and doesn't mean for my mother to call me, now, from a coastal cemetery. What it means—it's a book for sale in Dublin in 2016 along the River Liffey—*Gaza Photo Album.* It's the pink and orange flowers. It's— along the River Liffey, all the blown up buildings. You, you drive to Connemara and feel the chill of sandstone stretching toward the sea. The green plants reaching through the cracks. And I am driving in my car, now, and I am listening to the desperate kingdom of love, and I am listening to heaven and to hell. Had I closed the bedroom window, had we spoken of the light? That softness wanting to surround. Still, the boy, the boy is dreaming.

**AM Ringwalt**

Georgia Mannion-Krase

## No crip flag (After Calgacus)

I read about a league of disabled fighters in 1321 who plotted a
mutiny in a lepper colony. They wanted to poison the water with
their weeping sores. The revolt was scotched but like Anne Boyer
says, *it is enough for it to have once existed in a dream.*

RISE UP! RISE UP! You armless many
with second hand blades squeezed between your toes,
RISE UP! You aching many
in violent, powerful, mal-odourous throes.

In every region, in every sea, deep in
the churning ocean where none can gather
no one makes a chant for me.

Flying torn at every seam
the flag for crips is warped in
Red and black and white and green.
Red and black and white and green.

*Can they not see my army?*
The handsome dead 'n' sick 'n' dying
that fight to the death for their lives beside me.

Spotted leopard dreams strike pock across the centuries.
It's too long, the taser cord that shivers and their machines never
run out of shocks to give.

We cry out 'The Children!' And the less the children are seen.
We scream out murder in the asylum and the more mad it is we
seem. They will make a graveyard and call it peace. They will make a
graveyard and call it peace. Bomb a hospital and call it merciful
release.

D Mortimer

# Bastards

Jerome sold a bunch of old Phil Andros books—*Stud*, *The Boys in Blue*, *Shuttlecock*, and *Different Strokes*—because he's flat broke. Last month, he parted with his beloved show poster signed by Ethyl Eichelberger, Peter Hujar, and Agosta Machado. Collectors pay big for queer 70s and 80s memorabilia. *Vintage.*

Rent has gone up again on Jerome's apartment, an old Polish flat on Milwaukee's lower east side bought by an Arizona-based management company. The letter announcing the hike had a land acknowledgment. "Does that mean I can pay the rent increase to the Ho-Chunk tribe?" Jerome said after he read it to me.

"I know it's hard but…" I forget the rest because we are seated outside and a man I used to fuck is nearby. He concertedly watches his dog root around in some grass.

"It's absurd. I guess I could have unloaded all this stuff ages ago. I thought maybe I'd pass it on to someone someday."

"Well, you did in a way."

"Desperation."

"Yeah, I know the feeling."

The man and the dog are gone. Johnny? Pickles? Lenny? Chuckles?

\* \* \*

Jerome says, "Once the antiviral drugs came out, it was like a gag order. People stopped talking about AIDS. *Here's your pills, shut up, faggots.* And we obliged. We were exhausted. Or I was."

Jerome turns sixty next month. He's $70,000 in debt. No house, no car, no vacations, no savings. Student loans and credit cards, with some medical debt heaped on for variety.

"Pay my serf fees and get a doughnut," he says.

HIV-positive since 1988, he was near death when the cocktail came along. My Lazarus. I try to remember the names of the treatments and medications he has been prescribed or is currently taking but it's a jumble—NRTIs, NNRTIs, INSTs, PIs. I forget if he's on Mercy Medicaid or Badgercare Plus Standard or if they are the same thing. At times, it has been a full-time job staying alive.

An old friend from his New York days is having late-life success as a painter and Jerome reads to me from the article: *"I'm living for all the people who couldn't. Everything before digital, there's now a push to erase. And I am insistent on not being erased." Erasure seems an unlikely fate for a character as vivid as Tabboo!, one who embodies a nearly extinct breed of artist whose daily existence seems to be an organic part of his practice.*

"What the fuck? Erasure is unlikely yet Tabboo! is part of a nearly extinct breed. Which is it? It's so typical, salute and nod at the past and race into the future. For two years, I woke up every morning expecting to see Kaposi's spots and now it's all a little context in an arts and leisure story."

Jerome is on an AIDS hit parade: Sylvester, Klaus Nomi, and reissues of Diamanda Galás records. I listened to her trilogy *Masque of the Red Death* back in the late 80s. At the time, she said, "My voice was given to me as an instrument of inspiration for my friends and a tool of torture and destruction to my enemies."

I hadn't revisited those early albums in a decade. I listened to the live recording *Plague Mass* Galás recorded after the trilogy. Its final lines are: "There are no more tickets to the funeral. The funeral is crowded!" The audience's applause and shouts at the end brought me to tears.

Galás is sixty-six now and lives in San Diego where she grew up. She moved back to care for her ailing parents until they both died. She rarely sees people. I relate to much of this. A kind of withdrawal. The world not as too much—as the agoraphobic spectrum is imagined—but as too little. Thin. Inconsequential.

When her mother died, Galás fantasized about painting the house's interior entirely black, covering the windows with duct tape, and soundproofing the structure so that she wouldn't hear anything from the outside. Extreme grief or an appropriate reaction to the world's noisy chatter? Stylized of course because style is always important even if no one sees it. Especially so.

I saw Galás on the street in New York, twenty-more years ago. She looked like Salvador Dali's wife dressed as the Empress in the tarot deck he was commissioned to make in the 1970s for the James Bond film *Live and Let Die*. The deal fell through, but he made the deck anyway (he cast himself as the Magician, of course). No matter. The Empress glided ahead of me, and I watched her. The late afternoon low sun in my eyes. I looked away and back. She had disappeared.

\* \* \*

No reason to stay, nowhere to go, no claim ticket, nothing.

Claude gripes about the changing (again) neighborhood. In the park where he liked to read and smoke a cigarette (Down to one per day. Quit? Never. Contain.), a shiny new sign prohibits *adults except those accompanying children*. A mother asked him to leave.

"Me. I've lived in the neighborhood for thirty years and these fuckers push me out."

He talks about his older friend, a mentor and once-lover, who has sundowners. The light changes and the shadows come alive. Mornings, still lucid, he shares stories about growing up in Westfield, New Jersey with its colonial graveyard. A favorite hangout of Charles Addams. It has the classic tombstone: *I Told You I Was Sick*.

The envy and malice of shadows watching our old world go and the arrival of a bright abyss. They ignore the debts we paid on the other side. Our currency has no charge, and our promises aren't broken because the language they were made in no longer exists. Too young to be codgers strolling time, but suddenly old, slipping verses, breathless to the chant of the new pledge of allegiance. Everything outside the hot spotlight is a vanished world.

* * *

You win. I say it all the time to people. You win. You won. You're the winner. Congratulations. I said it when a boyfriend told me he didn't love me. I said it on the ward. I said it when I got the notice to cure. You win. Good for you.

* * *

Young friends badgered Claude into attending drag brunches in hopes he'd photograph them. What he saw was boggling. Gymnastics and bombast. Drag as a defanged little clown school. He remembers Bloolips, Leigh Bowery, Charles Ludlam, Vaginal Davis, Joan Jett Blakk. Gleeful derangement. Undomesticated rage.

"Isn't that progress though?" a friend asked.

"It may be for some greater good—that nebulous pink cloud— but I assure you it is a disaster for individuals."

* * *

You know the opposition: they urge you to forget.

Claude was an abortion clinic escort and in Queer Nation, Jerome was in ACT UP and served a jail stint for a nuclear protest. Would anyone believe it? Most of them would see—if they noticed at all—a Jurassic table standing in the way of the future. When will they die? Soon, baby. Maybe even at the same time as you.

I was in the ratty queer punk scene. A handful of misfits hellbent on escapist fun and sexual mischief more than politics. I'd volunteered for various gay and lesbian organizations and been treated like shit by the slumming college kids and scolds enough to know I didn't need another place to not belong.

We recall apartheid protests at the Capitol rotunda demanding the university to divest in South Africa, watching CNN as the bombing of Baghdad played out like a distant town's fireworks—a perfectly stage-managed war. Now images are everywhere, and people claim what you're seeing has been doctored, falsified. Your lying eyes. It's like being a Catholic boy all over again.

\* \* \*

Digital displays promise eternity—a hurtling world that doesn't need your lurching and inefficient mind. The body is the flaw in such a system but maybe soon enough someone will figure out how to solve that problem. Who needs to watch television or see another movie or play a video game or spend an afternoon online? Walk outside and watch people move and interact. They are so deformed it's no longer necessary to experience the source material. Faces are screens, people are aggregators.

Most people I encountered in the old world are unrecognizable to me now. Prosopagnosia but of values, love, stories, histories.

The article title: How will you be remembered?

I hope not.

\* \* \*

I tell Jerome that Jean Rhys is my favorite queer theorist: "I do not feel gay but rather frightened. Not 'rather' either."

He quotes Camille Roy, who he's been reading: "Sometimes I feel that the truest respect one can show towards the past is to allow it to be something other than a predecessor of the present…"

Claude sends me a great interview with Rabih Alameddine: "I feel like more of an outsider than I feel gay. The more the gay community gets co-opted by the dominant culture, the more I feel like a double outsider."

\* \* \*

Jerome and I cater together—a cash gig. We're the scummy fags serving the queers with expensive degrees and little status kinks in beautiful homes.

"We're being wiped out more efficiently than AIDS. Friendly fire," Jerome says.

The depoliticization of the word queer offends him. The term has been drained of anything radical and just become a Tupperware container for kink-shaming hall monitors, marriage-and-mortgage conformists, and HR careerists freaking out over public sex at the Folsom Street Fair. Identity has been elevated over what people do—actual deeds. Conformity has changed names.

"Everyone is queer now. Half of them are little prudes talking about eliminating sex scenes in movies, bringing back the Hays Code for fuck's sake, calling everyone a predator or a groomer—they sound like the wingnut Christers, but will shout you down as a gatekeeper if you don't agree. They will tell you nothing is queerer than the pregnant body, they use it as a verb, queering the canon, queering Crate & Barrel."

"Yeah, I've given up. Last few years my close friends have shrank down to mostly other effeminate gay men our age. We were the queers, now we're the homosexuals."

"It's so depressing."

"I understand how it got here and I don't want to be the identity custodian. guess I want to be left alone."

"Jesus."

"It's the natural order. We're old and it doesn't matter what we think. As a kid told me, *You were born in the 1900s.* We are last century. A new world is here."

"At least we have our health."

# Untitled

when the abuser

has his boot

upon the neck

of the victim

he will have much

to say

to justify himself

he will

have many

stories

to tell you

prepare

yourself

do not

abandon

Palestine

whose fists

are raised

in rubble

whose children

pack their bags

and repeatedly

try

to walk

to school

Ruby Lawrence

Elektra KB

The one is never enough. Its glare is monolithic, or transparent; a stare-down or an invitation to absorption. Oftentimes I see them singularly or together, not knowing which I prefer – or need. But if the shifting clouds of harmony are capable of interrupting the heartbeat, why would I want the lone note? Perhaps because no such thing exists. A note intones, rings – the proverbial bell, gong, or tam-tam; myriad frequencies reach out further and further into reverberation. Does it end? Or does it join other phenomena in a circuit of the senses, sound morphing into colour, colour into plastic form? Call it synaesthesia, one sense stimulating another. Harmony of the spheres? Those lengths of strings connecting one body to another can twist and turn. Frequencies and forms modulate. We are overcome. There is movement from the outside to the inside. And then a going down and an in-dwelling.

It could be that I never cared to separate the tones of the mix. A fool's errand: the darker the colour, the greater the challenge it is to know the which from the what. Please leave your binaries – dark and light, black and white, this and other – at the door. Protect me from the gungy palette from which mysteries are divulged. Concealment of admixtures is my colour theory.

The lone note vibrates, signals its potential for harmony. Gaps are eliminated. Give me my *diabolus*: that forbidden, awkward interval making resolution all the sweeter in the end. That's supposed to be the promise anyway. The decision is equally mine: I conduct the contrasts without melding them. Those gaps, discrete and narrow, spring me like a coil. Taut promise of that which stands.

Christopher Madden

## How "Never Again" Happens Again

Swear
it's in

God's
playbook:

Bomb
a(way) to

someone-must-pay
safety

and democracy.
Cage

the neighbors,
convince

the world
to disapprove

resistance—
audition for

empathy
denied.

Fashion
history into

an everlasting
noose.

Exhaust
everything

to groom
enemies

then commence
a pageant

of victimhood
when

the human animal,
heel on neck,

fires back
its pain.

Pretend
desperation

that ignites
the present

isn't present.
Gaslight

the cleansing
from those

who once felt
its water:

"We can
never

forgive them
for forcing

us to kill
their children."

|

A baby's
family

gets smashed
like glass.

Complicate
how

she is
no longer

anyone's
daughter,

sister,
or niece.

Her worth
summed up:

the quieted crime
confers her

right to be
exterminated.

A minister
relishes

the uses of
the dead.

Once
the cage

is
an urn,

proclaim
victory.

## Notes

"audition for empathy" from the original title of by Dr. Hala Alyan's essay, "Why Must Palestinians Audition for Your Empathy?" published in the *New York Times* on Oct. 25, 2023. The title was later changed to "The Palestinian Double Standard."

"human animal" – Israel Defense Minister Yoav Gallant said, "We are fighting human animals, and we are acting accordingly" in a speech on Oct. 9, 2023, after declaring a complete blockade of the Gaza Strip, where no food, water, or electricity may enter the Occupied Territory in response to a Hamas attack on Israeli on Oct. 7, 2023.

"We can forgive the Arabs for killing our children, but we can never forgive them for forcing us to kill their children," said by Golda Meir, former Prime Minister of Israel.

Daniel W.K. Lee

# YOUTH: STATESIDE

there is a pervasive, cruel attachment to "feeling historical", i
text james, who replies, and it is a misremembered feeling, yes,
of course, and mark messages that he is very scared, which
makes me think of my mother, who is very scared for me
because i live in a jewish neighborhood, then june posts, i just
have to say... that "all lives matter" ish post everyone has been
sharing makes you sound like a midwest mom like grow up,
which we all kind of knew was true, and i loved that tweet, if i
had to go to an IR class at american university today i would
[redacted], the comments made me laugh even if it was
macabre, like when beatty joked, if we don't see eye to eye on
this issue rn we will def never have sex, and i go, rip sontag you
would've loved to have written 9/11 as metaphor, but then the
group chat would get serious, and puck texts, it's one thing to
say hamas' actions aren't "justified" - but to say they're not
"explainable" ??? now he's sending the hamas press conference
and gill asks, do u think most americans care if u.s. empire kills
non-white people, no, that's the reality, answering their own
question, and i text everyone, the self-censorship bothers me so
much, just as nate interjects, why do so many people think i
and others care about what they personally think about what is
going on, but, pucks says, i wouldn't be an antizionist if i didn't
start as a zionist who wasn't afraid to say it and be challenged,
and, lia replies, no one has a problem announcing they are
implicated in white supremacy, which was so right that it made
me mad again, and i write, too anxious to post lol... you
pathetic fucking babies—wait - it's gill again - oh my god has
anyone checked on heba, yea did u see the gofundme? puck
sent a link, and i tell beatty on the phone that ahmed sobbed
after he fucked me last night, it's just so so awful, and i can
literally hear the protest in the background as she walks to a
class on grief, we say what we are both thinking: will anyone be
able to make it through?

Daniel Napsha

## Asperity

Cacophonous    ,        ;        ssss
       a stertorous puffing fain to augment
every hold        every sold        gainsay admonitory        tones
       impute a farouche laxity ,        [*a scalloped map*]
the gimcrack of ones outrage        disquietened.
       Asperity. Hues of distempered polishings.


Mediascape. Pressure built up        ; non        -        alignment,
       erstwhile dispositions, disposed of dirty words,
contiguous geographies and architectonic faults.
       A pre-verbal imputation. Exhort. Impress upon.
Conjugate said paradigm. "*Do the work.*"
       Sat it out, this one. What's it all about, anyway.


Image.                        Life.
       Form extant.
Polity.                        Exhaustion.
       Vacuum.
       *Scenes of the Occupation In Gaza* (1973).
Here and Elsewhere.
       The Wolves.
"        *What are we for*        –        "
       Faultlines
Social intercourse.

Ossified ideology.

         Anti   –        |————|

Multipolarity.

A muddying structure of violence     – Begetting

         A Fragmentation.

Grandstanding.

         A Retreat.

Manichean moves.

         Clash.

         Bondage.

The Afro-Asiatic incursion.

         *Protect our possessions.*

*The Jewel in the Crown.*

Acute doggerel.

         Chyme gusseting up.

Perception, isnt.

         I wither.

**Kashif Sharma-Patel**

GREENREDBLACKWHITEGREENREDBLACKWHIT
GREENREDBLACKWHITEGREENREDBLACKWHIT
GREENREDBLACKWHITEGREENREDBLACKWHIT
GREENREDBLACKWHITEGREENREDBLACKWHIT
GREENREDBLACKWHITEGREENREDBLACKWHIT
GREENREDBLACKWHITEGREENREDBLACKWHIT
GREENREDBLACKWHITEGREENREDBLACKWHIT
GREENREDBLACKWHITEGREENREDBLACKWHIT
GREENREDBLACKWHITEGREENREDBLACKWHIT
GREENREDBLACKWHITEGREENREDBLACKWHIT
GREENREDBLACKWHITEGREENREDBLACKWHIT
GREENREDBLACKWHITEGREENREDBLACKWHIT
GREENREDBLACKWHITEGREENREDBLACKWHIT
GREENREDBLACKWHITEGREENREDBLACKWHIT
GREENREDBLACKWHITEGREENREDBLACKWHIT
GREENREDBLACKWHITEGREENREDBLACKWHIT
GREENREDBLACKWHITEGREENREDBLACKWHIT
GREENREDBLACKWHITEGREENREDBLACKWHIT
GREENREDBLACKWHITEGREENREDBLACKWHI
GREENREDBLACKWHITEGREENREDBLACKWHI
GREENREDBLACKWHITEGREENREDBLACKWHI
GREENREDBLACKWHITEGREENREDBLACKWHI
GREENREDBLACKWHITEGREENREDBLACKWHI
GREENREDBLACKWHITEGREENREDBLACKWHI

Anne Tallentire

*In Zuccotti Park I walked amongst sleeping bodies as the sun slowly rose. Wall Street suits curiously observed the sleepers as they sipped their morning brew.*

*I began filming before sunrise, aside from the stray car alarm and the squeaking of bus brakes, the city was silent.*

*To see so many bodies at rest with one another spoke what could not be written on a banner: the image of strangers at ease, together, no longer separated by walls, dreaming.*

*As the slumberers rose from their sleeping bags they watched the office workers move in pressed suits, both saw the other as spectacle.*

*I watched them all, for months I biked to the park whenever there was a hole in my day. It was exciting to know that wherever I was, that here, the protests continued.*

*One day I brought a camera, to watch the day come to life, to see how the collective bloomed only to again find rest, publicly, in a city that we were told never slept.*

*When I think of that time, I think of a poster, carried by a man in a white suit, his hair short and white, his mustache perfectly trimmed.*

*His sign,*
*written on white poster board:*

*"Be Someone Else Sometimes."*

Dylan Angell

## The drawbridge rising and the follow-through

Grief is the sound of the horse who wants for water in the cities.

I was in that city. In the scaffolding, the city's

Sutures, I picked up the slack left
By the lazy version of me confronted

With death. I said, That's not me

Flinching in integrity

In the bar
In the hotel's bar
In the bar's hotel
In all of the bars of all of the hotels

I could not find a room to answer

If I could get there I would
Pick up the slack left by the city

And I would call that a display.

Katherine Franco

# Choke

Where does history go when it's choked? Flag banned, two million caged, their existence an inconvenience, hidden away. I will go to the doctor tomorrow and try to articulate something about my mental health while genocide occurs live on TV. A Palestinian is denied that complexity — must be rational, calm, turn the other cheek, accept the blame for their annihilation. Where does empathy go when you choke it down? When you cite complexity to excuse your lack of courage? When you annihilate four colours lying next to each other, think you can lock them away like two million people in a cage, pretend the combination does not exist? In the occupying nation, every tragic death gets a name, a history, for the occupied, there are too many bodies to count, too much red. What if I ignore all this and concentrate on self-care? Then self-care would be the choking of my humanity. All love is hollow if we let this happen, hollow if we don't try, the heart just a hunk of bloody meat.

Len Lukowski

## Orange, red and yellow

Real voices on the radio
From the Artificial In Telephone
Real faces on the tele
Are Lit Like Marilyn

Both saying: *she*
Then saying: *them*

Resourced enough to no

But more is more and longer is more
And your no is no'd
Even to know is to not

On the Artificial In Telephone
Stuck to the dashboard
And the Lit Like Marilyn
Which shines from the wall

I saw a video where a boy says
"I dream of eating sugar"

And another child
"I dream of seeing my mother and eating bread"

It clarifies the noise and glare

Grey microfibre faces,
Wearing the shell of a woodlouse,
Are flecked in sunrise paint
Like pieces of fruit
Which sweeten and wet their clothes

Grey microfibre faces kiss,
Scratching and stretching
Finding hardly intelligible lips.
It tastes like clementines
Roses and damson jam
Like orange, red, yellow

And a green night sky
Colours flown across
A white LED lit globe
Serving sugar and bread
On brick dust plates
Some will never know

Turning on the Artificial In Telephone
To watch them Lit Like Marilyn

Cyrus Larcombe-Moore

## solitary consciousness

time's unfurling like a banner in grand
central station. days of desperation
settle in a haze over ev'ry city.
in this still-twinkling universe i need

to believe that each murdered morning
opens a heavy gate in space:
primal, strange & waiting.
on the other side

cowboys sip vanilla
dunkin & fuck each
other gently; dead kids dream
in beds of fudge & velvet deep

& love is everywhere hot
& tangled like spaghetti ~

Sophie Robinson

# Trails

put down a deposit down and then
a surveyor says its unliveable
it's different and it's the same
someone says its unliveable

they'd do it here too

the mouth a gash in a plastic bag
  a still small liquid voice of calm
Begging. Pleading.
Shouting.                in the eulogies
they'll say things like "promising"    call it
"aid" without a ceasefire

they'll do it here too

grass yellows to die
          guides us

          Poems songs do such brutal things.

---

They, who reside in the passive, keep divvying things up. We
must set things side by side. There are certain facts, the facts
condition, intersect, and glance right off our language. Like
the great oxidation event, or the 1981 Wimpy bombing, or
Suella Braverman's concern over some chants, or the
Cambrian explosion, or a tweet from Mira Mattar, or the
destruction of Al-Ahli Arab Hospital, or the new season of
Frasier. We'll build anthologies of facts so varied their
stupid world will cave in on itself, the world of warmongers
murderers, their facts our facts side by side like rubble like
grass like ash. Do you feel that?

24/10/23

Robert Kiely

# roses and daisies and forget-me-notes

In the family album at home there was a card sent by my grandfather to my grandmother during the first world war.

On the front was a photograph of a golden dome. Inside was a pressed flower from Palestine where he was serving. It was like tissue paper, still faintly flushed pink with the sun it had known.

I used to look at this card long and hard. I felt the flower was under the dome. Something so precious that it had been sent over the sea all the way to England. As though my grandfather had worn it in the buttonhole of his khaki uniform.

*

Lounging in his decadent boudoir in Carchemish, Syria, in the heat of noon, in the sort of room Oscar Wilde longed for, Thomas Edward Lawrence, a young archeologist fresh out of Oxford, wrote his name in a new book he had received from Berlin,

*Der Tod in Venedig, T.E.L., 1913*

The story was the result of Thomas Mann's obsession with decadence, youth and death. Whoever recommended it to Lawrence knew what they were doing.

Lawrence had long held a deep romance of the Near East. At Oxford he had sought out a Palestinian professor to teach him Arabic. He wanted to escape all those dreaming spires and water meadows, for a place that would test his soul.

*

Two years before, in Beirut, 1911, Lawrence had met James Elroy Flecker, a dark and handsome young man then serving as a diplomat, but who was also a protegé of John Aldington Symonds, the first man to use the word homosexual in a book. Lawrence already knew Flecker's lover, the tall and languid John Beazley, who was a poet-archeologist at Oxford. There the duo of Beazley and

Flecker had been inseparable and notorious for their provocative stunts and their secret club.

The town wasn't big enough for them. They were photographed together as bright sparks, wearing overcoats and shorts.

It was a memorable look. You can imagine them dancing on a podium.

Flecker introduces Beazley to healthy sports

It was inevitable that Lawrence would want to join their gang. Flecker was a keen cyclist, charging around the south coast of Hampshire from his family's summer house at Southbourne, with its view of the Isle of Wight and its back to the New Forest. Lawrence had grown up nearby, in a house by Southampton Water, where he learned to swim.

Lawrence was fascinated by Flecker, who was of Polish Jewish descent. He represented an intimate if not erotic route from Oxford to the exotic of the Near East, as if it were only a step away.

A tantalizing place to leave the confines of Europe for; to be, well, frankly, gay.

Flecker's poetry gave all these emotions away. When they read them, Flecker's parents banned Beazley from the house. Meanwhile Flecker continued to write poems to other mysterious lovers, such as the anonymous dedicatee,

G.T.B., *Drowned among reeds at Wisbech.*

These young men posed such emblematical questions that you might think Oscar had invented them. He had, in a way. Flecker is a god in shorts, a Dorian Gray too darkly good-looking for his own good. An advertisement for men's grooming products. His black hair only makes his vivid blue eyes stand out even more.

I had rather be told that I had beautiful eyes than that I pulled all the wires in the university, he said.

*

Flecker catches us in the flicker of those eyes. Who could fail to fall in love with them? In his most celebrated poem, 'The Golden Road to Samarkind', written in 1913, he imagines the journey there, fitting his gaze to these words of yearning,

always a little further, it may be,
Beyond that last blue mountain barred with snow
Across that angry or that glimmering sea.

The sea that raged no more. Flecker's poem echoed the shores of Utopia upon which Oscar was also arriving, like the alien he was, and from where he was always setting off. Forever restless, Flecker saw,

old ghostly ships: that sail like swans asleep
Beyond the village that men still call Tyre

as if he knew he would always be leaving, too.

The packing must have been a chore. His Oxford rooms were filled with
mountainous piles of rare books, strange fruits, bottles of liqueurs, curious
nicknacks and pictures in luxuriant disorder.

There is something barbaric about you, a friend told Flecker, when I saw your
taste for those lurid pictures: the monstrous shapes: the weird castle on a steep
impossible cliff: a blue obscene moon leering from a purple sky.

It was less a reprimand than a love letter.

In decadent Berlin Flecker learns German. He is sent to Beirut as a diplomat.
His body is already infected with consumption. The light of the future is on his
face. But it is fading fast.

He wasn't built to last. Lawrence comes to visit Flecker in Beirut, where the poet has assumed loose Arab dress.

Lawrence has brought his camera, and poses Flecker in costume, standing on his balcony.

Flecker holds his robe around himself as though he'd just stepped out of the bath. His feet are naked in his red leather slippers. A rug is flung over the balustrade for privacy.

Lawrence adjusts his lens for his friend.

Flecker came here for his health. He liked to be beaten, too.

J. E. F., by Lawrence, on the Balcony at Areya.

He is a model for what Lawrence would become.

Photographs won't save him. His lungs are as affected as his verse. Soon he'll be consigned to another balcony, on the Swiss Alps, in the snow.

It's an experiment in time and space.

The mountains are a retreat, like the desert, like the sea.

Stranded up there for his own good even though there was no hope, Flecker, homesick, dreams of Southbourne's pine trees, planted there for the health of its own consumptives.

> When, lonely boy beneath the chosen tree
> I listened, with my eyes upon the sea.

*

In December 1913, Flecker writes to Lawrence, recommending books. Among them is Mann's *Death in Venice*, published that year in Berlin. A sensational story of the love of an older man for a young boy in a time of cholera. The same disease that was even then sweeping through Carchemish.

Do write me a word, Flecker writes. I'm sick and very miserable, he says.

It is his last postcard, sent from his cruel mountain-side in Switzerland, as Lawrence would recall.

Flecker's final address is a tubercular sanatorium in Davos. He dies there, aged thirty years old. Thomas Mann is staying a similar establishment in same town.

*

In 1908, Flecker had written a speculative novel, The Last Generation, set in a future state, in which a man named Joshua Harris has become King of Britain and Emperor of the two Americas, making proclamations in a huge elliptical hall bigger than the Coliseum, lit by a thousand electric discs attended by an International Police Force in tunics and boots.

Birmingham has become a city which never sees the sun or the moon, and a Vertilgungsverein has been established in Germany, a Club for Mutual Extermination set up by Teutonic scientists disappointed by the evolution of the human race.

No one would imagine how the badge on the white, gold-edged blazer which Flecker still wore from the club he and Beasley devised at Oxford would change in meaning, embroidered as it was with the swastika, the ancient sign of mystical Eastern divinity, worn on his Jewish breast.

*

At Carchemish Lawrence keeps a snow leopard for the winter. The house is furnished with rugs from the market and a Morris tapestry from Oxford; the curtains are red leather. He wants to melt Roman glass on the walls to give it lustre, like a jewel in the desert.

He swims every day in the Euphrates which turns his hair even more golden as it dries and is burnished by the sun. No one has ever seen such intensely blue eyes.

He wears a blazer of French grey trimmed with pink and a gaudy Arab belt with white football shorts, long grey stockings, red Arab slippers and no hat.

His hair was very long and in wild disorder, said Woolley, and it used to get in his mouth at mealtimes.

His constant companion is Salim Ahmed, a young Palestian nicknamed Dahoum by his friends, the little dark one. He and Lawrence try on each other's clothes.

The Arabs are tolerant of the friendship, says Woolley, even Lawrence brings Dahoum into the house to live with them. Woolley insists his friend had a remarkably clean mind. Greek homosexuality interested him, but in a detached way. Like everything else.

Lawrence gathers roses and daisies and forget-me-notes for the house, and writes about the handsome young Arabian men whose clean limbs quiver on the yielding sand as they lie clasped together. Like Roman centurions. He sleeps naked under a blanket in the desert, to test his resolve.

He always felt himself beyond the law, and, as Woolley adds, he liked to shock. He takes Dahoum back home to Oxford like a tapestry or a shard of Hittite pot.

Look what I found. Dahoum's broad smile is bewitching. They sketch him in the Ashmolean Museum like a living exhibit in a vitrine. Lawrence knows perfectly well what people think. He doesn't care.

When they return to Palestine, Dahoum saves Lawrence's life three times.  Then the war parts them both.

Five years later, Lawrence, now the "hero" of Arabia, learns that Dahoum has died of typhoid.  As he tells a fellow soldier the news, Lawrence draws his kuffieh over his face and says,

I loved that boy.

When he turned back, it was clear that he had been crying.

In 1922, Lawrence publishes his *Seven Pillars of Wisdom*.  It is dedicated

    To S.A.

I loved you, so I drew these tides of men into my hands
        and wrote my will across the sky in star
To earn you Freedom, the seven pillared worthy house,
        that your eyes might be shining for me
                        When we came.

S.A. was a person, now dead, regard for whom lay beneath my regard for the Arabic peoples, Lawrence told a friend. I don't propose to go into further detail thereupon.

He was the only person Lawrence ever loved, said his friend.

*

The card with the pressed flower and golden dome in our family album vanished long ago, like so much else. But for years, when I lived in London in the nineteen-eighties, going out dancing and getting lost in myself, I'd come back to my ninth-floor council flat and sleep under a blanket my grandfather had slept under in the desert.

I found it again this week, as I pulled things out of a cupboard. Damp had pressed it into felt. Mottled and brown. It was useless now. I laid it on top of a cardboard box.

And I went down to swim in the sea, which was dark and misty in the hours before dawn.

24 October 2023

Philip Hoare

# Four boring rectangular canvases

I wanted to show my partner the Rothko Room at the Tate Modern, one of my favourite places in the city, but the exhibition has closed, and they won't be here until the beginning of 2023. Before, when it was open, I would go there whenever I went to the Tate. I would look at rectangular canvases, specific slants of light hitting them in particular ways, and only hope that I could follow in the direction that they seemed to gesture.

The colour(s), shade(s) of The Seagram Murals, in what was once the Rothko Room, are not forbidden. I see a variation on this colour on the quartet that Félix Gonzalez-Torrez says some will define as *four boring rectangular canvases*. They are a gesture, a whisper. An attempt to make bright, concrete, and immovable an image that, even now, decades later, on the precipice of erasure.

I get a DM on Instagram from a friend telling me that a post of hers I liked - another gesture, another attempt to create something solid, solidarity - was taken down. I find myself imagining those four rectangular canvases somehow becoming less rich with colour, less layered with meaning; as if each act of erasure - something that begins with simplicity, with a post taken down - could reach through time and take away what we must remember. Like someone fading out of a picture in a science fiction film. Maybe, if I keep my eyes locked on those four rectangular canvases, they'll have to stay, have to keep speaking to me, letting me offer, if nothing else, an echo.

Sam Moore

## *My Love Wears Forbidden Colours*   (half a glosa)

As you conduct your wars, think of others
  (do not forget those who seek peace).
As you pay your water bill, think of others
  (those who are nursed by clouds).

(Mahmoud Darwish)

White                              (deeds)


*Life believes in you once again*   believe

in life right back and set yourself the task

of revolting       so we may know we are

not just think that we are       reach out a hand

*as you conduct your wars, think of others*


Green                              (fields)


*My hands in the soil*       waking from

a dream of return                to find earth

of the fields on me       in my mouth

filling in my       fate line       life line

*(do not forget those who seek peace).*

Red                    (swords)

*Wounds on your hands never seem to heal*          weeping

wounds your eyes that see through time      weeping light

time in rubble              stopped      caked in dust and light

*walking in circles*              to tunnel a way out

*As you pay your water bill, think of others*


Black                  (battles)


Beat of my heart          scroll back

*senseless years thunder by*

think of us                    we are here      still

*a lifetime away from you*

*(those who are nursed by clouds).*


Ellen Dillon

# With The Morning

with the morning, easy things
like light over a pane —

the glazing of it,
the grazing of it

there will be a morning
held at home

not soon, not worth any of this
never worth, never

but there must be a morning
promised rather than threat

that might only be a matter of waking,
holding something or being held, or not

easy logistics
like hell

there will be a morning
so there can be hope

when hope again is something
too true to be awful

as mornings remain possible,
even if they're dreaded

even if unwatched
or unwatchable

there will be a morning
so there can be hope

Eley Williams

# A Garden, While Waiting

Morocco. Beginning of the 80s.

There is a river. The Bou Regreg. And the sea. The Atlantic Ocean.

There are two cities. Rabat, the capital. Over there. Far. White. Rich. Inaccessible. Salé: our side, my side. City of pirates, of privateers. Of the poor.

There is the world. The idea of the world and its boundaries, so visible, so internalized by everyone.

Where can we go when we have nothing? Where can we walk, wander, when we are nothing?

It takes some time to understand that the earth and the sky belong to everyone. To me, too. To my mother, crying. To my father, who smokes too much. While waiting for this revelation, we do what we can. We go back to the forest. We get lost. We try not to exist anymore except as bodies.

And one day: the miracle happens. On our side, without consulting us, they build a garden. For everyone. With benches, a lawn, some trees, and even a basketball court.

Bewilderment. This is for us, this space? Really? They haven't made a mistake? It's not for the people of Rabat?

At the beginning, we snub the garden. We're not used to such things. We don't know how to inhabit this new territory or what to invent to familiarize ourselves with its architecture. Its geography is not our own. Its organized void is destabilizing. Distancing. Its benches exude a bearing that we lack.

We don't like it, this garden. We refuse it. We exclude it. We forget it. Several months.

My childhood friends and I continue to play barefoot on the ground, in the dust. That's us, this contact with the elemental, the "savage." We have to stay like that. We have to resist the ideas of others, those on high who don't know us and don't come to see us, ever.

We decide to stay in our territory. Let it die, their sophisticated garden! Let it be burned by the sun, by boredom! Let it disappear! We don't want it! Do you understand? Yes? No?

The poor must remain poor. It won't be a so-called modern garden that releases them from the poverty imposed upon them and constantly covered up by those in power.

We have understood. We will not let ourselves be had. Resistance is underway. It will continue. Always. Always. Have you understood?

Time passes. A year. Two years.

The children grow up. I'm thirteen. I become a man. Another boundary to cross. But I don't want to become a man like the others order, demand. I am different. Homosexual. But, in the end, I don't feel different at all. I am poor among the poor. No differences. I don't want to leave this group. This world. I don't go to the garden either. So where is the difference? I don't see it at all. But the others, my family, my friends, some adults, see it quite well. They say it. They shout it.

What to do? Fight? Cause a scandal? Hang my head?

I choose the third option. I am pushed little by little toward solitude. The void. The garden.

I stop talking. And I start to wander. I go to the garden. I still don't like it. But I go there anyway.

I discover that I'm not the only one who goes there. The elderly also go in the afternoon, after the third prayer. Men in their sixties worn down by our violent society, done in. Rejected. Loveless. Awaiting death. They play cards, again and again. They invent something else.

I approach them. I watch. I become attached. I go to these meetings more and more often.

I am young. So old. With these patriarchs, sometimes, there is happiness. Bursts of laughter. Tender gestures. They give me advice that I never follow. But I listen to them. I sense their fears. Their frustrations. Their solitude. They no longer have the force to resist. They wait. Like all of Morocco. I feel...solidarity. And my underlying feeling is confirmed. I am homosexual but I am not different from these men.

The old men gave me a place among them. They saw who I was. They said nothing.

One night, I'm alone in the garden, I linger. Night. Darkness. People come. They're holding cheap bottles of wine. I watch them. They're far. Transgressive. Drunks. Bums. Prostitutes. I'm not afraid. I go toward them.

I resist at their sides. Simply. Naively. Lovingly.


*Translated by Emma Ramadan*


**Abdellah Taïa**

Mary Manning

# Couple

"...one must see many cities, men, and things, one must know the animals, one must feel how the birds fly and know the gesture with which the little flowers open in the morning."

- Rilke, "Blood-Remembering,"
trans. Mood, in *Felix Gonzalez-Torres*, ed. Julie Ault

*Green Land*

The writer Jean Genet saw seven greens: green slope, green houses built on piles, used when the soil is lacking firm strata, green shutters, green palms, a green bug, green card carried by every fedayee, green painted fingernails. The flag flying in public would be banned again. In September of '72, the white writer was in Beirut when Israeli invaded, when it disappeared under the bombs.

*Guns in Black and White*

A sheet from a sheave, stack, printed with all the faces of people killed by handguns in the U.S. in one week was tacked to the wall over across from

the bed we shared, 460 that week, a piece from 1990, a year before
school, years before I flee to New York City. Newspaper print. We part
mornings and there comes a point in the day when scrolling includes
popping up of pins on a map of Gaza: the imagination of ever holding
hands gone, who you did not kiss before you will soon be dead. A target.
I am reading Mishima, the green of *Wicked* on Broadway, the MTA fare
machine, the green LED saying time and place and the tiles around the
subway stop. Meanwhile, there is a war, I keep saying.

Maybe sex is inconsequential.

In the chapter of *Forbidden Colors*, the "windows appeared red...by the
neon light." I keep advancing to the white and not focusing on the black.
Revolution remained isolated, pitch black. Coordinating with area
hospitals. Electricity inside the busiest hospitals cut. The snow-white bed
was empty.

*Easement*

Two green plastic buckets in the camp,

or make them red, monochromatic, fear doubles.


'88, the year of Gonzalez-Torres "Forbidden Colors" painting—panels

coming together to form the work defined by a current moment's hold as

well—would also be the year he made his first stack piece—on white

paper on a pedestal one of his timelines printed out for you to take away.

And '88, his first graph piece, based on results of his blood work (a bead

curtain installation, *"Untitled" (Blood)* comes in 1992, Clinton horizon),

before more white and black paintings of blood test results: acrylic, gesso,

and graphite predominating, photographs and paper layered also in as

part of one of the works, two final ones no gesso, one with wax in its

place.


88, he made a framed photostat with five dates interrupting some

ubiquitous staples of my childhood, guns and religion and who they said

was going to infect us all. The year everyone (but two) in the Senate said it was okay if people like me died, if we had sex. The NRA does not want anyone to have to wait seven days to buy a gun. The year of Kennedy's assassination. Today: Person of interest ID'd, shooter, and coordinating with area hospitals. You are reflected back in the glaze, the nominal "Gaza Strip" part of a running typeface, white serif, black field.

White border around a red square that holds black words, *WE DON'T REMEMBER*, in German. Red paper with a black border, NRA. Red paper with a white border, "National Front."

A carpet made of green candy is the hotel where we hid out. He has made a bed for them. Room by room, I walk through the MoMA's Geffen wing. I pay my taxes and my taxes go towards guns, weapons. In 1990, the artist notes an explosion of the information industry and implosion of meanings, numbers unthinkable, white deeds. In 1990, the artist notes growing racial and class tension. "Ideology cannot stand it when we make connections." The bright lights gather in the corner or hang from the ceiling, hang from the ceiling to pool on the floor. Across my device the day's horrors coming, secondhand flutters. I count bulbs spread out entwined, bulbs as body positions. Body that is or isn't a platform. (I am reading Yogita Goyal, anticipating a visit, quoting the Afropessimist position of Frank B. Wilderson III: any analogy to blackness (for instance, to Native Americans or Palestinians) is... "mystification" and an "erasure" because "grammars of suffering are irreconcilable.") Triggered incursion.

If I see the sculpture as a clock face, I am standing at 9 o'clock. Crossed wires. Bulb count forty-three? Clockwise, counterclockwise. From 6 o'clock I reach the same sum, forty-two in going around again. Count again, lights on a beach got to or not.

Douglas A. Martin

## October in Neukölln

Green

nowadays    to make oneself into a proper European    to keep
    passing as one
        you must learn well    never
           to say the word *Palestine* let
        alone anything of its freedom

Red

This is a list—still accreting in its wreckage—of what the German state and
their local police have lately forbidden, upon penalty of beating, detention,
water cannon, arrest, deportation, misdemeanor or criminal charge,
expulsion from school, obstructed participation in public events and cultural
exhibitions, financial retaliation, including the severance of funding,
chokehold, & being dragged down the street while an officer uses his hands
to shut your eyes, mouth, and nose simultaneously (lest you scream the name
of someone who has been bombed to death in Gaza):

wearing a keffiyeh at school
wearing a keffiyeh on the street
any public commemoration of the Nakba
the Palestinian flag
Samidoun, a solidarity network for Palestinian prisoners
the "Demo for a Free Palestine" that was to take place in Neukölln, a
    working-class district in Berlin where many Palestinians have come
    to live
a demo calling for a ceasefire in the Middle East
a demo in "Solidarity with Civilians in the Gaza Strip"
a demo against "Violence Against Children in Schools"
lighting small candles on the street to mourn Gaza's dead
saying out loud at a protest that Israel has murdered children
stickers bearing messages of Palestinian liberation
a rally registered under the name "Children in Gaza Need Help"
support for the Boycott, Divestment, and Sanctions movement
wearing what the police have described in their reports as "typical
    Palestinian clothing"
an assembly of "Youth Against Racism"
shouting "Free Palestine" on the street
another protest advocating for "Peace in the Middle East"
a demo called "Berlin Children for the Children of Gaza"
standing with a friend on Sonnenallee while smoking a cigarette, in what
    a police officer interprets to be a potentially illegal assembly

any kind of pro-Palestinian motorcade

basically, almost all public gatherings in solidarity with Palestine (in parallel with France, whose interior minister declared that all pro-Palestinian demonstrations must be "prohibited because they are likely to generate disturbances to the public order" and, further, that any foreigner whom the state declares to be anti-semitic should be "immediately expelled")

any pro-Palestinian writing mounted in public spaces (police rove the city and transform such inscriptions until they are "unrecognizable"; they also erase drawings of Handala, the cartoon kid who stands with their back turned toward us until the day Palestine is free—and is named after حنظل, a plant that grows back whenever it is cut)

a public assembly of "Jewish Berliners against Violence in the Middle East," which was cancelled on the grounds of being anti-semitic (White Germany, in exquisite hypocrisy, has made itself the world's arbiter of anti-semitism—with the power to say who the perpetrators are and how they should be punished. History comes full circle in this prerogative to prosecute Jewish people who say of the war, *not in my name*—for being a threat to themselves.)

being present at an assembly that the police have forbidden just shortly before they arrive to announce it is forbidden, and proceed to take off their badge numbers in order to apply excessive force in anonymity

any "substitute assemblies" for those that have been banned

"*suspected* participation in a prohibited assembly"

at demos, the word "genocide" to describe the genocide

a demo against the cancellation of demos

the chant "from the river to the sea, Palestine will be free"          it will

White

Interdiction is the least creative act. Predatory in practice. Broker than broke in spirit. It functions solely to impede possibility. When European settlers landed themselves in the New World, they prohibited enslaved people from reading; owning weapons; playing the trumpet; testifying in court; striking gourds; meeting up to grieve and bury their dead; wearing any "costly finery"; blowing conch-shells or large horns; taking on the dress of mourning; and, among other things that bring life a little closer, performing the ring shout (a sweaty dance that some speculate derives from the Arabic *sha'wt*—a circular, counter-clockwise procession around the Ka'bah in Mecca).

With a litany of interdictions, the settler-class attempts to ban the life out of the occupied. And to reduce its captives to an existence papered over in prohibition. The furious proliferation of forbidden things is a show of dominance that belies desperation. A settler's ban is always late—gasping, coming after what is already socially manifest. And—it is often petty. In occupied Palestine, Israel does not only impose severe, systematic restrictions of movement but has also outlawed small-scale activities of sustenance, like foraging for the wild green akkoub. As a means of enforcement, Israel has deployed state forces to surveil and chase after dispersed people, many older on in years, who were walking the land, collecting these small plants by hand, as has been done for generations.

In the punishing fluency with forbidding language—which knows no magic, only force—the mind of the settler unites with that of the fascist. One of the only pieces of legislation that was carried over from the Nazi regime, unchanged, was Paragraph 175, which criminalized sexual acts between men. Under the purview of its enforcement, German authorities imposed a *Tanzverbot* [dance ban]—appointing armed fleets of police to patrol the city, just to make sure that no two men were dancing with each other. Immense force directed against subtle pleasure.

Against themselves, the settlers' long dossiers of forbidden things provide a hardened and partial archive of the generative power of the subjugated. By its own logic, colonial interdiction believes itself to have the final word. But often it is just the beginning of another way through impossibility. Wherever the Palestinian flag has been banned—as it is now, still and again—watermelons fly. When, in Trinidad, the British colonial administration forbade Black captives from playing the drums, they started instead to percuss on old car parts, trash lids, and oil barrels: & in the ruins of prohibition came the first sounds of calypso.


Black


                              [this palpable drop, reminiscent of the thirties]
it is a fact that, after Israel declared its war on Palestine, the German chancellor was swift to announce that finally the time has come to begin large-scale deportations. it is a fact that the anti-semitism of the West cannot be regurgitated, one migrant at a time. it is a fact that young people in Gaza are writing their names on their bodies, so that if they are killed, their remains can be identified. it is a fact that Biden publicly doubted the very death count that he exerted great power to augment. it is a fact that numbers cannot approach all that was lost to Gaza while the leaders of Europe sat, debating whether they should call for a humanitarian *pause* or a more meager *window*. it is a fact that, when i wrote to sarah ihmoud, she said, *habibi, the grief is unbearable and we are each doing what we can but it feels like we are just screaming into the void*



                                               come sundown,
          i am taking a watermelon for a walk down sonnenallee i will
meet her there, and we will pass the weight of its irrepressible colors between
                                                      our hands


                                             **M. Ty**

from the river to the sea

Mark Armijo McKnight

# Children

Of light, that is,
Making other people see the,
At the end of the tunnel,
Which burns film,
Which causes a squint,
Which bleaches art and textiles
Paintings and flags,
As in the colours of physics all at once.

And of darkness, that is,
Furtive, possible,
A place to hide,
A place someone else might hide their secrets,
Paint colours all at once,
The flag's tippy-toe reach.

And what of the children
Worlds away, Worlds away
Who in a gallery
Dare to see,
In a well lit room
Full of shadows and of licks,
Holding their father's hand?

Jack Sagar

# Contributors

*In order of appearance*

Cecilia Pavón
Ben Estes
So Mayer
Eileen Myles
Paul Lee
jimmy cooper
Lucy Swan
Davide Meneghello
Chris Jones
Matthew Kinlin & Neil Davies
Hesse K.
Prem Sahib
William Butler
Alistair McCartney
Richard Porter
Kathy Pendrill
Richard James Hall
Ashleigh A. Allen
AM Ringwalt
Georgia Mannion-Krase
D Mortimer
Nate Lippens
Ruby Lawrence

Elektra KB
Christopher Madden
Daniel W.K. Lee
Daniel Napsha
Kashif Sharma-Patel
Anne Tallentire
Dylan Angell
Katherine Franco
Len Lukowski
Cyrus Larcombe-Moore
Sophie Robinson
Robert Kiely
Philip Hoare
Sam Moore
Ellen Dillon
Eley Williams
Abdellah Taïa
Mary Manning
Douglas A. Martin
M. Ty
Mark Armijo McKnight
Jack Sagar

*Responses to Forbidden Colours (1988) by Felix Gonzalez-Torres*

100% of the proceeds from the sale of this publication will be donated to Medical Aid for Palestinians

Published in the U.K. by Pilot Press

978-1-7393649-4-6

Printed on 100% recycled paper